GOD IS FOREVER

Brown Bear and Red Goose have two children, a gosling named Charity and a cub named John. They all believe in God.

God Is Forever
2012

All rights reserved. No part of this book, including the illustrations, may be reproduced or used in any form without written permission from the author.

Copyright William Lane Craig

ISBN-13: 978-1480038004

ISBN-10: 1480038008

God Is Forever

The Attributes of God for Children

One day Brown Bear and Red Goose took Charity and John for a walk.

"Papa, can I ask you a question?" said Charity.

"Sure, Sweetheart, what is it?" said Papa.

"Where did God come from?" she asked.

"The Bible answers that question," said Papa. "It says, 'Before the mountains were made and even before You made the world, from everlasting to everlasting You are God'" (Psalm 90.2).

"What does 'everlasting' mean?" said John.

"It means that something lasts forever," said Papa. "It goes on forever and never comes to an end."

"And the Bible says God is everlasting," said Mama.

"Yes," said Papa. "It says God is *from* everlasting *to* everlasting. That means God never had a beginning and will never have an end."

"So where did God come from?" said John.

"He never came from anywhere," Papa answered. "God never began. He has just always been there. God is forever."

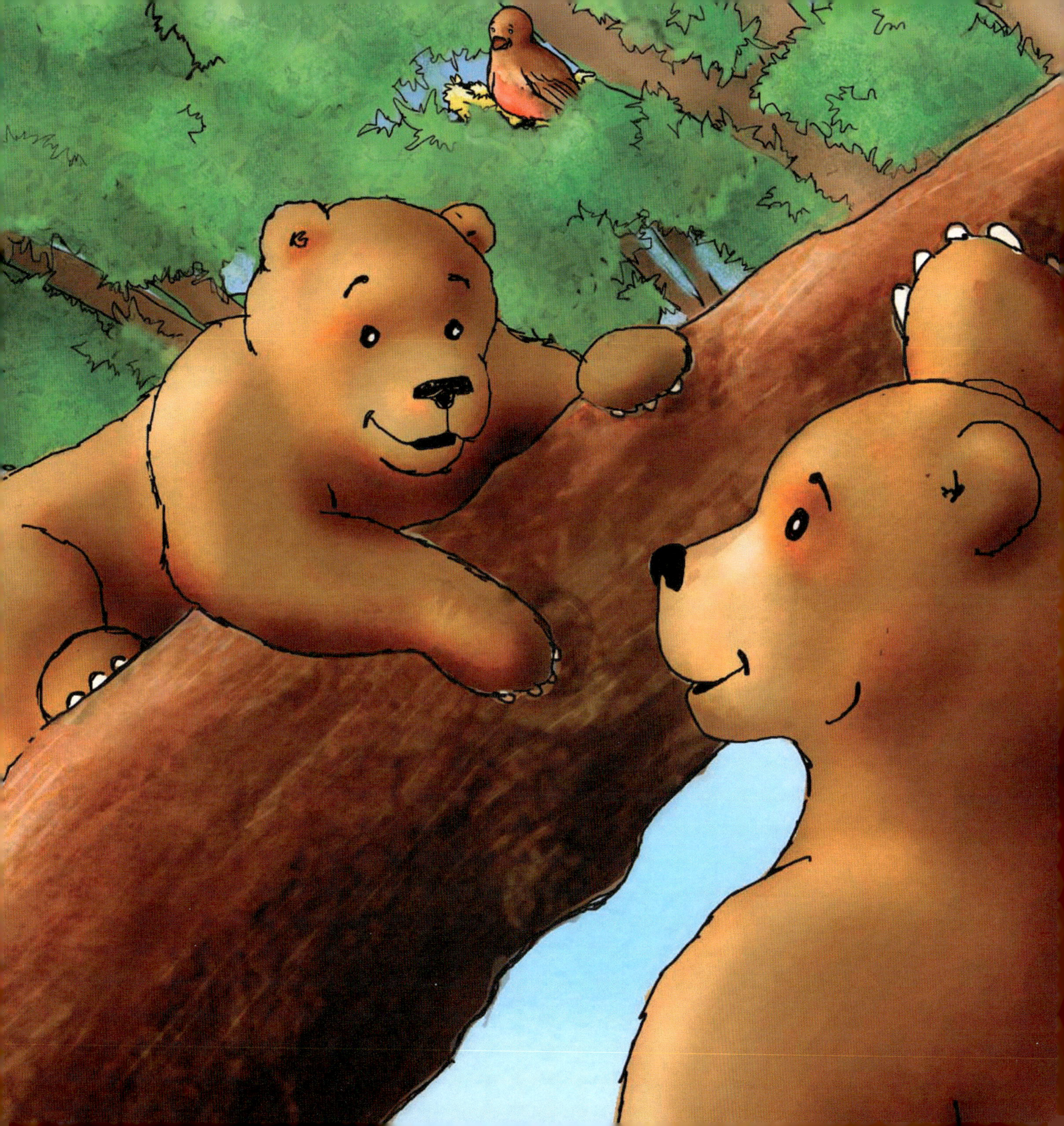

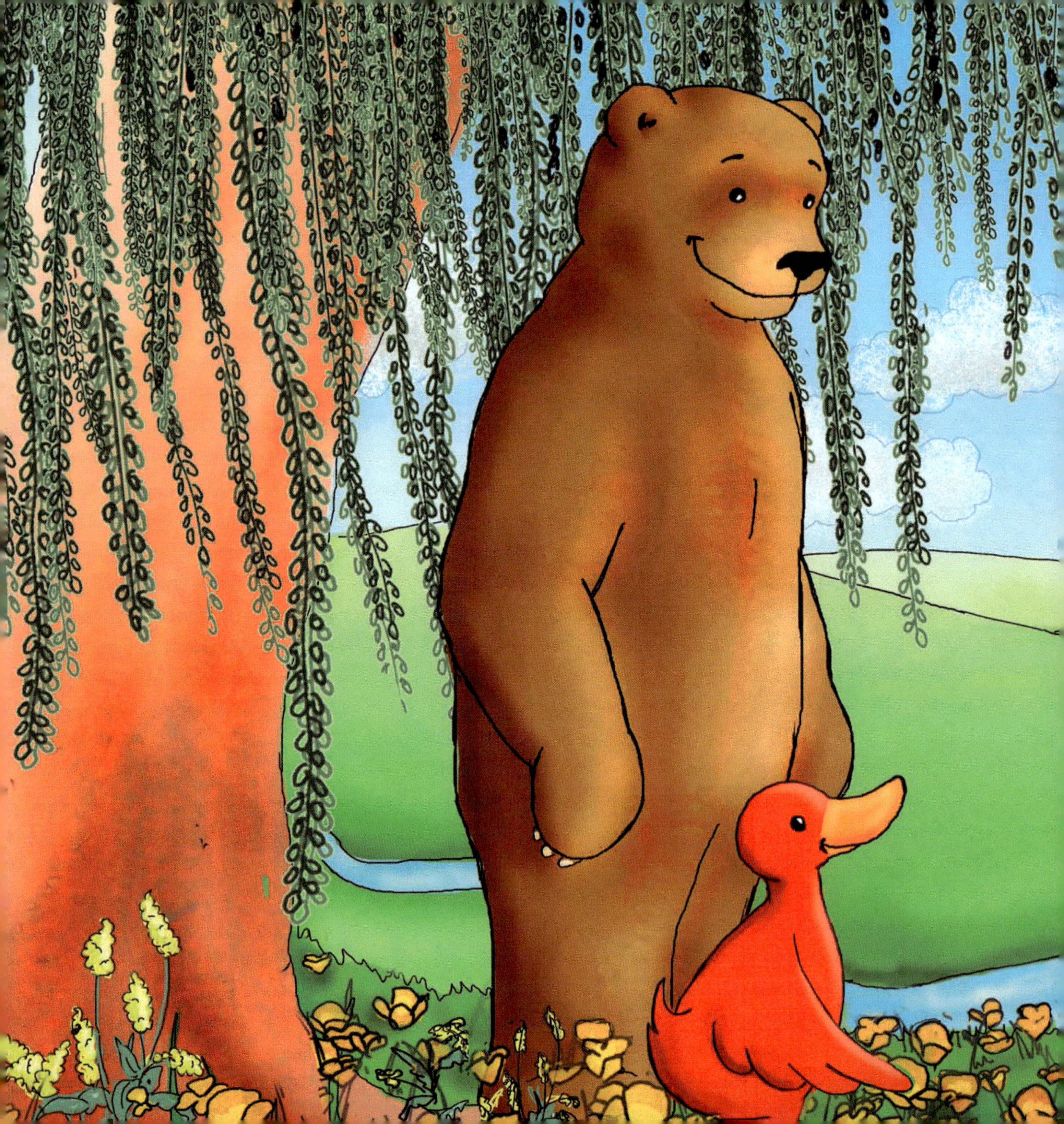

"But the world began, didn't it?" said Mama.

"That's right," said Papa. "God made the world, and before it began there was nothing except for God."

"Will the world end, too?" Charity asked.

"The Bible says that when Jesus comes back, *this* world will end, and God will make a new world for us to live in forever," said Papa.

"So we will live forever?" said John.

"Yes, if we believe in Jesus," said Papa. "We will live forever with God."

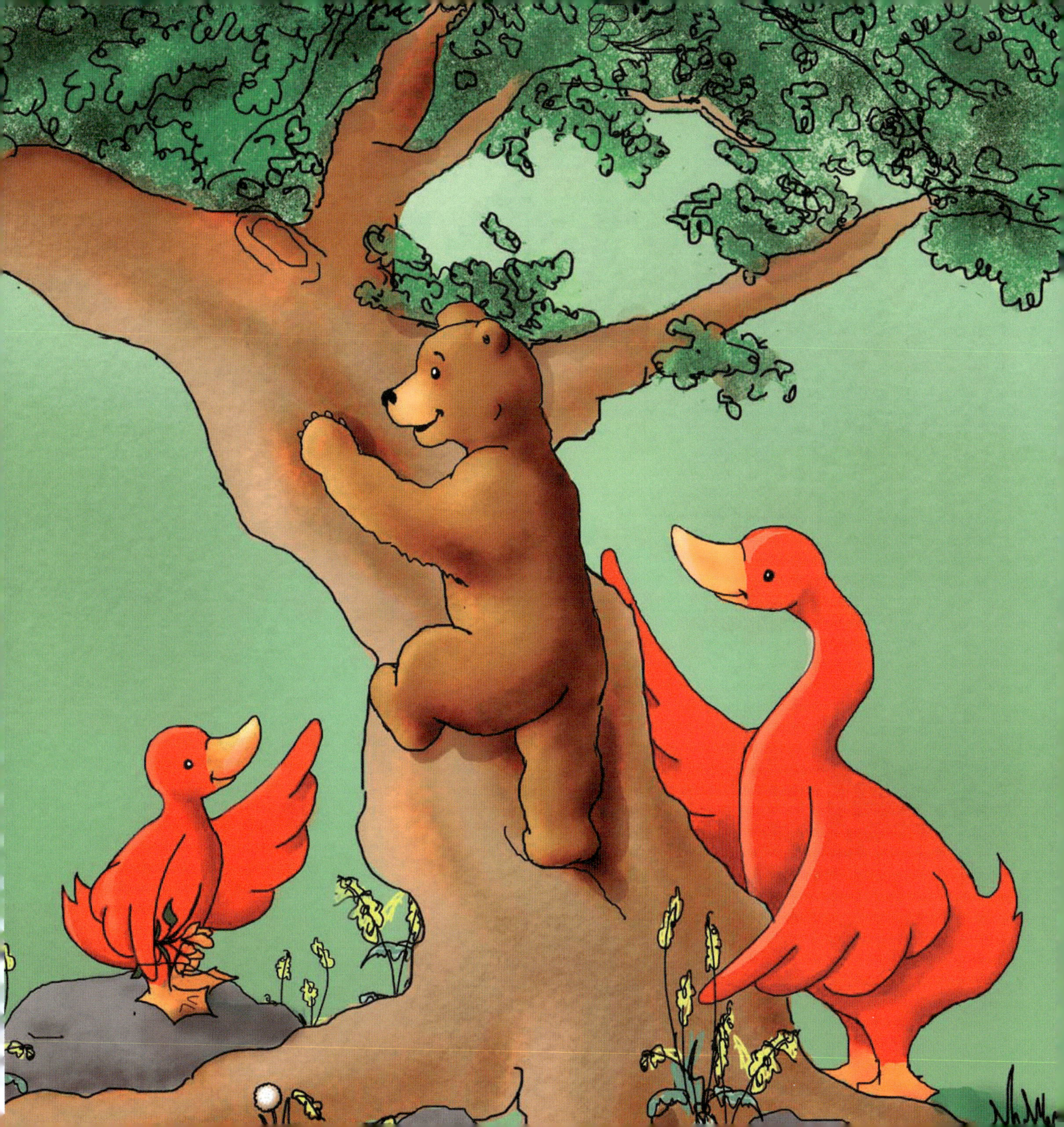

"It's nice to know that God is forever, isn't it?" said Mama.

"It sure is!" said John.

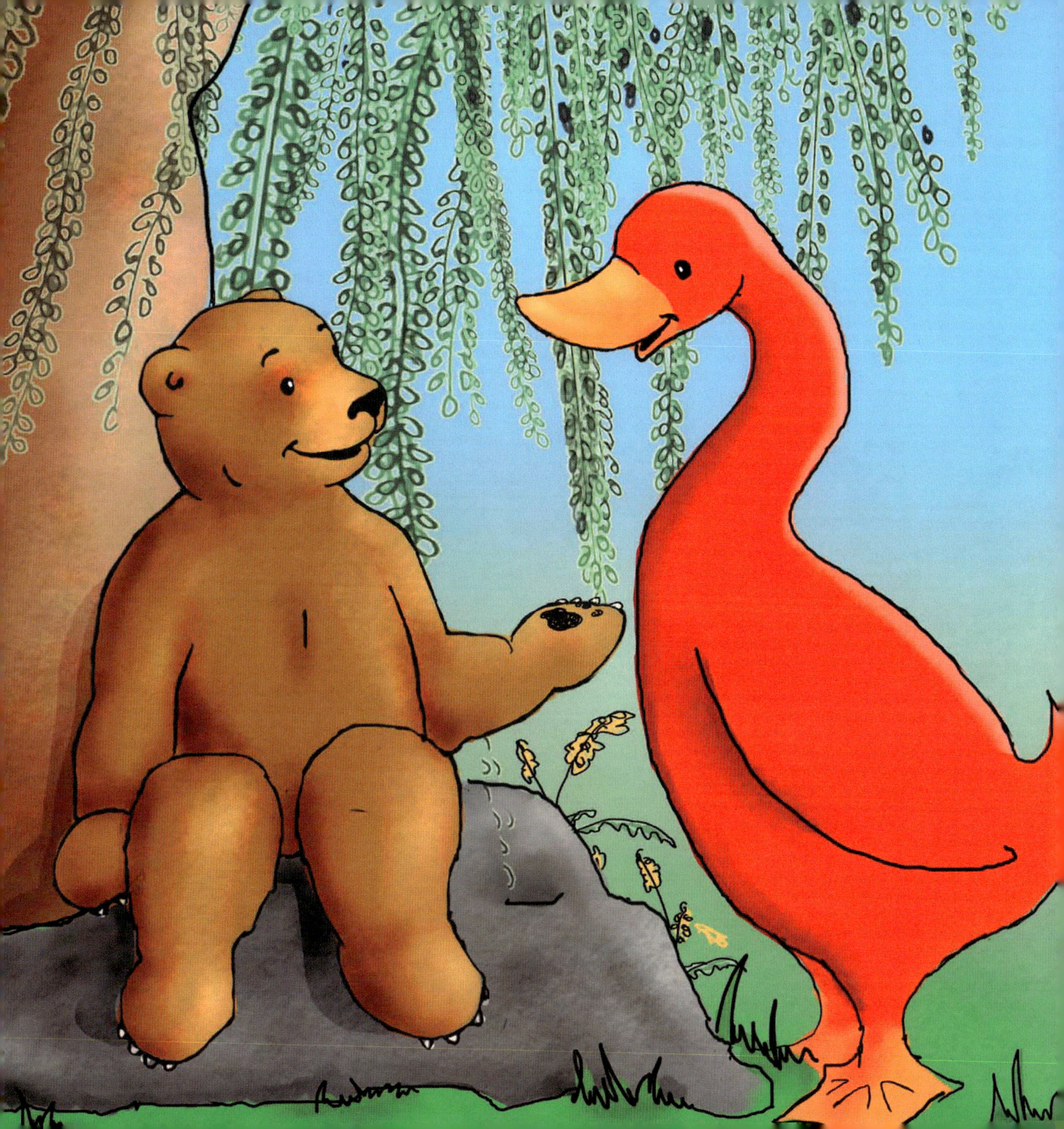

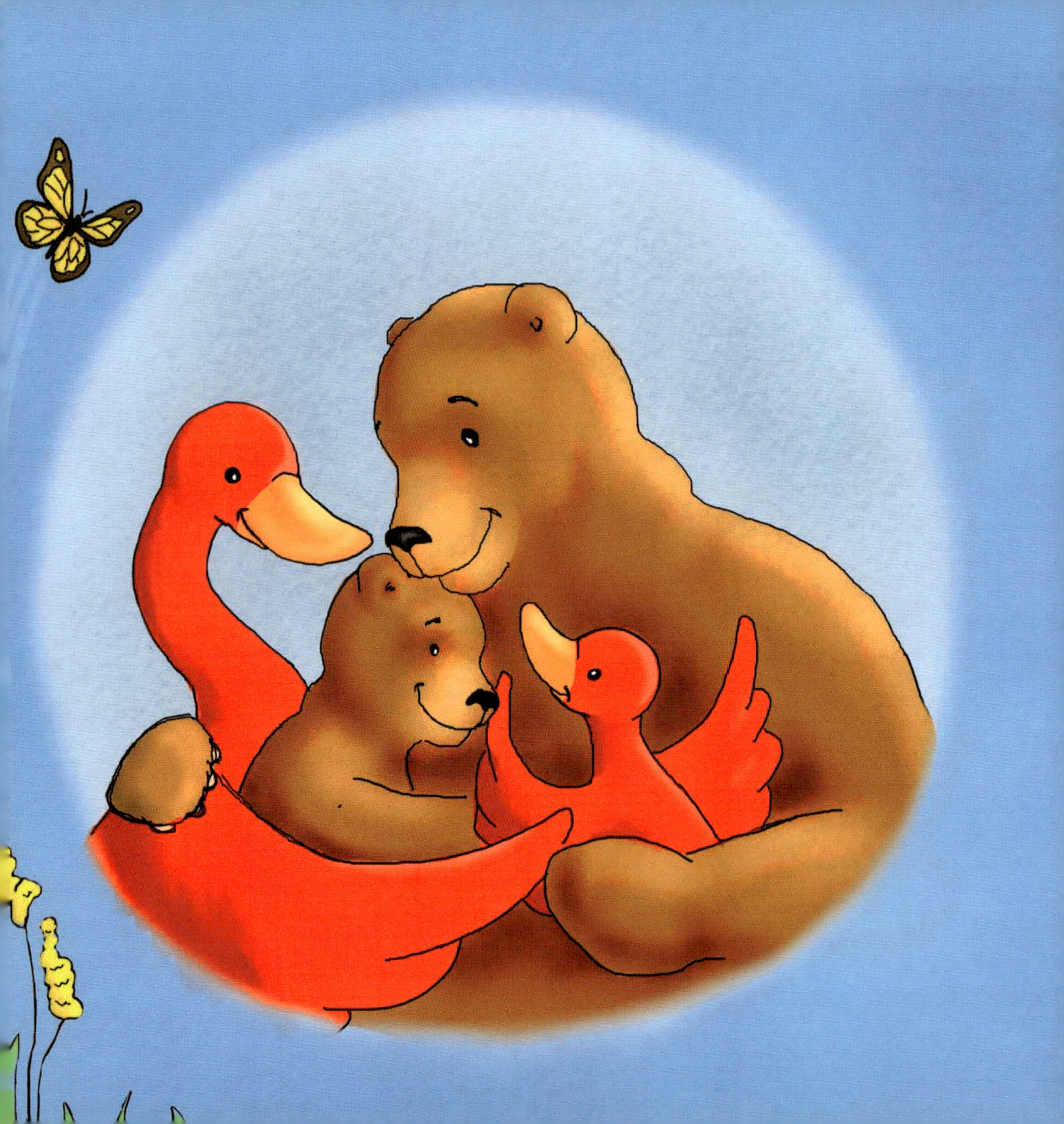

"It makes me feel safe," said Charity.

"Me, too," said Papa and gave them all a big hug.

Memory Verse:
"From everlasting to everlasting You are God." – Psalm 90.2

Books in the "What is God Like?" series

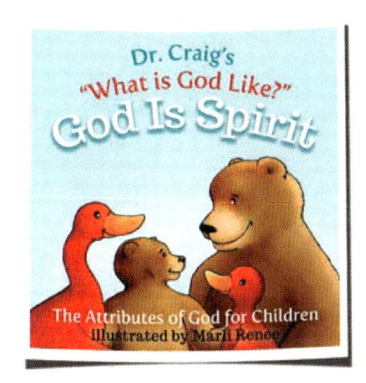

I. God is Spirit

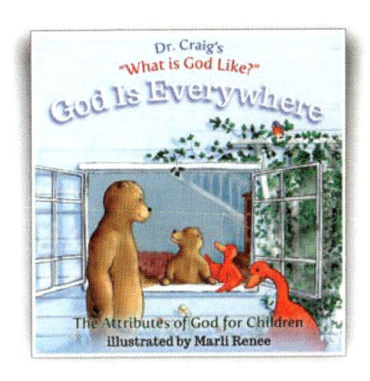

II. God is Everywhere

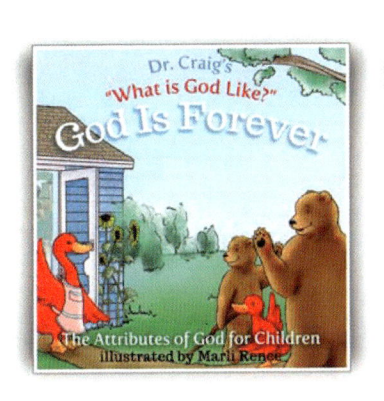

III. God is Forever

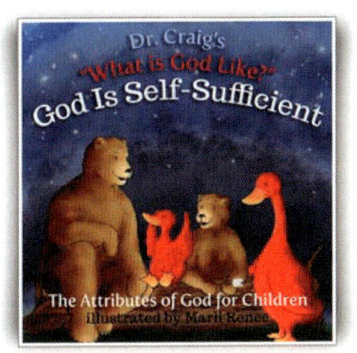

IV. God is Self-Sufficient

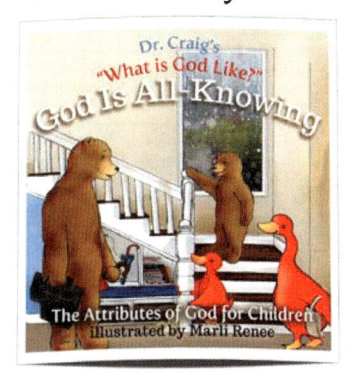

V. God is All-Knowing

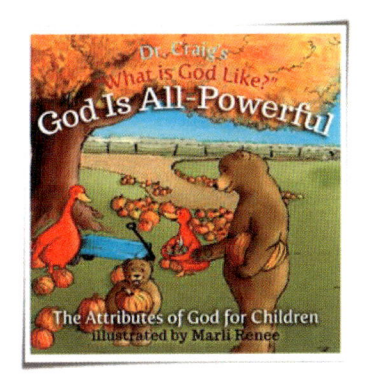

VI. God is All-Powerful

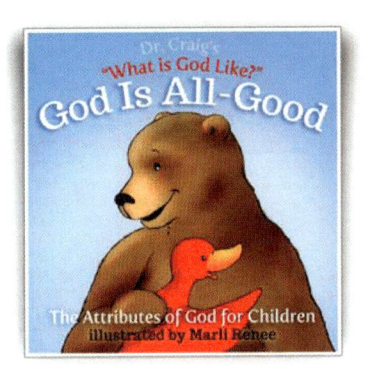

VII. God is All-Good

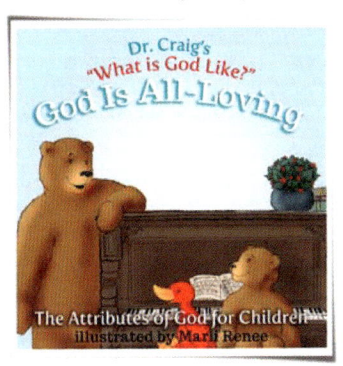

VIII. God is All-Loving

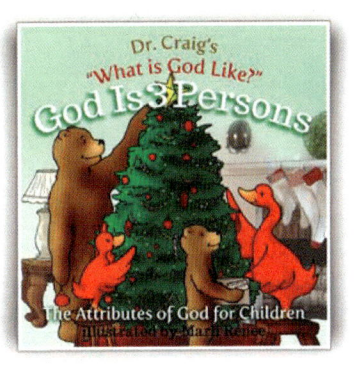

IX. God is Three Persons

X. The Greatness of God

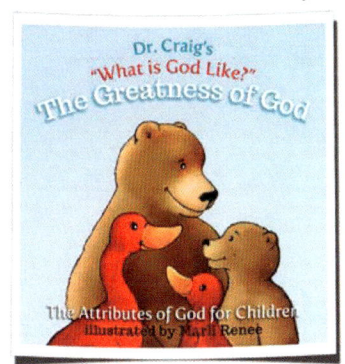

Ready to go deeper?

THE DEFENSE NEVER RESTS
A Workbook for Budding Apologists

A fill-in-the-blank workbook on Christian Apologetics and accompanying teacher's handbook

William Lane Craig
& Joseph Tang

Available at www.ReasonableFaith.org/DNR

"In these pages, you'll learn the most compelling arguments in favor of Christianity. You'll discover that *On Guard* is solidly factual, winsomely personal, consistently practical, and ultimately convincing in its presentation of the case for Christianity."

- Lee Strobel, former skeptic and author of *The Case for Christ* and *The Case for the Real Jesus*

ON GUARD

Defending Your Faith with Reason and Precision

WILLIAM LANE CRAIG

BEST-SELLING AUTHOR OF REASONABLE FAITH

On Guard and *On Guard Study Guide* are available at www.onguardbook.com

Made in the USA
Charleston, SC
07 December 2013